The Poetry Book Society
Anthology 3

The Poetry Book Society Anthology 3

Edited by
William Scammell

Hutchinson
London

This edition first published in 1992 by Hutchinson
and by the Poetry Book Society Ltd,
10 Barley Mow Passage, London W4

Random House UK Limited
20 Vauxhall Bridge Road,
London SW1V 2SA

Random House Australia (Pty) Ltd
20 Alfred Street, Milsons Point, Sydney,
NSW 2061, Australia

Random House New Zealand Ltd
18 Poland Road, Glenfield, Auckland,
New Zealand

Random House South Africa (Pty) Ltd
PO Box 337, Bergvlei, 2012, South Africa

A CIP catalogue record for this book is available from the British Library.

ISBN 0 09 177351 2

Typeset in Times by Edna A Moore,  Tek-Art, Addiscombe, Croydon, Surrey
Printed and bound in Great Britain by Cox and Wyman Ltd, Reading

Contents

Introduction

British poets gave themselves a bad press in the 1960s and
1970s. Compared with glamorous Americans walking the
razor's edge, and heroic East Europeans battling against
oppression, we were genteel, dull-and-provincial, stuck in a
King's Road of the mind somewhere between Kipling and the
Children of Albion. Larkin was worshipped by some,
derided by others, Betjeman much the same, and Hughes
the same again. We'd apparently lost a poetic empire and
not yet found a role anyone could agree on, except as
snappers-up of our own bewilderment.

Morrison and Motion's *Penguin Book of Contemporary
British Poets* (1982) attempted to restore confidence and
steady the boat, pointing to the Northern Ireland renaissance
and to new talent in Britain as a whole. But the lineaments
of the book itself, as physical and mental object, were
thought by many to gratify only stunted desires.

Outside London the consolidation of Carcanet Press (and
PN Review) in Manchester, and of Bloodaxe Books in
Newcastle, seemed to open up new possibilities, and
incidentally to confirm the nation's pluralism, or its
polarisation between the academic-conservative Right and
the right-on liberal Left – Davie and Sisson versus Bunting
and Harrison. Other small presses and magazines flourished,
as did the Arvon Foundation, and the confidence of poets in
Scotland, Wales and 'the regions'. *Poetry Review* was
revived under Peter Forbes. 'World Poetry', that rather
dubious top-ten entity, conjuring a new MacSpaunday out of
Heaney, Walcott, Brodsky, Murray, poured in on us from
all quarters, and English poetry reconnected itself – if indeed
it had ever severed the link – with vital national and
international concerns.

This thumbnail sketch of the past 20–30 years leaves much
out of account, of course, but points forward to what is I
think undeniable, namely a flourishing contemporary poetic
culture with something of the *brio* and the ambition once
thought lost to the novel and to more exciting poets
overseas. In this necessarily limited selection I have tried to

demonstrate the strength and depth of several generations of British poets, and in particular to exhibit the work of new or newish talents whose poetry seems as interesting to me as anything being written in America or Europe. If this sounds complacent or inflationary, as it will to some, I would argue that a degree of exaggeration is pardonable in the face of so much recent self-protective irony and 'satire'. High talent is as rare as ever it was, but that is no reason to denigrate or undervalue the renewals currently under way.

Alongside British and Irish poetry there is a selection of foreign poetry in translation which sets the local achievement in some sort of European context, and which has its own intrinsic interest. I could have wished for more space in order to make this aspect of the anthology less skeletal and arbitrary, but anthologies, like blood cells, have budgets to abide by.

I regret the absence of some names from this book, but poets don't write to order. My thanks go to the Poetry Book Society, to Anthony Whittome of Hutchinson, and to all the poets represented, for their help in making this selection possible.

William Scammell

ACKNOWLEDGEMENTS to Bloodaxe Books for permission to use the poems of Ottó Orbán and György Petri; to Harvill for the poems of Jaan Kaplinski and Aleksandr Kushner; to Gallimard for the poems of Paul de Roux in his book, *Poèmes de l'Aube*; to Garzanti for the poems of Attilio Bertolucci; to Penguin Books for the poems of Yehuda Amichai; to *London Magazine* for permission to reprint Douglas Livingstone's 'A Darwinian Preface'; to Oxford University Press for permission to reprint the poems of Jo Shapcott; and to Faber for 'Black and White' by Susan Wicks and 'Ice' by Simon Armitage.

Note on Guest Poets

YEHUDA AMICHAI was born in Würzburg, Germany in 1924, and now lives in Jerusalem. His *Selected Poems* is published by Penguin.

KATERINA ANGHELAKI-ROOKE was born in Athens in 1939. Her books include *Beings and Things On Their Own* (1986) and a translation of *Under Milk Wood*.

ATTILIO BERTOLUCCI was born near Parma in 1911. He is one of Italy's most distinguished poets, and father of the film director, Bernardo Bertolucci.

JAAN KAPLINSKI was born in Tartu, Estonia, in 1941. His collections in English translation are *The Same Sea In Us All* (1990) and *The Wandering Border* (1992).

ALEKSANDR KUSHNER was born in Leningrad in 1936. He taught language and literature at night school for many years, and was, like Brodsky, a member of the circle that gathered round Anna Akhmatova. He has published eleven collections of poetry, and translated Larkin.

DOUGLAS LIVINGSTONE, born 1932, is a marine biologist who lives near Durban in South Africa. His books include *Eyes Closed Against The Sun* (1970) and *A Littoral Zone* (forthcoming).

OTTÓ ORBÁN was born in Budapest in 1936. His *Collected Poems* appeared in 1986, and *The Cosmic Cavalier* in 1990. A selection of his work is forthcoming from Bloodaxe.

GYÖRGY PETRI was born in Budapest in 1943. A selection from his five collections of poetry, *Night Song of the Personal Shadow*, was published by Bloodaxe in 1991.

ZSUZSA RAKOVSZKY was born in Sopron, Hungary, in 1950. A selection of her poems is forthcoming from Oxford University Press.

PAUL de ROUX was born in 1937 and lives in Paris. He has published seven collections of poetry. *Poemes d'Laube* was published by Gallimard in 1990.

LOUIS SIMPSON was born in Jamaica in 1923 and later became an American citizen. His *Collected Poems* and *Selected Prose* are published by Paragon. He is Distinguished Professor of English at New York State University.

YEHUDA AMICHAI

Sandals

Sandals are the skeleton of a whole shoe,
the skeleton, and its only true spirit.

Sandals are the reins of my galloping feet
and the *tefillin* straps
of a tired foot, praying.

Sandals are the patch of private land I walk on
everywhere I go, ambassadors of my homeland,
my true country, the skies
to small swarming creatures of the earth
and their day of destruction that's sure to come.

Sandals are the youth of the shoe
and a memory of walking in the wilderness.

I don't know when they'll lose me
or when I'll lose them, but they will
be lost, each in a different place:
one not far from my house
among rocks and shrubs, the other
sinking into the dunes near the Great Sea
like a setting sun,
facing a setting sun.

tefillin: Phylacteries (two small boxes containing scriptural
passages, fastened with leather straps to the arm and
forehead during morning prayers, in fulfilment of Deut. 6:8).

At the Seashore

The pain-people think that God is the god of joy,
the joy-people think that God is the god of pain.
The coast dwellers think that love is in the mountains,
and the mountain dwellers think that love is at the seashore
so they go down to the sea.

The waves bring back even things we haven't lost.
I choose a smooth pebble and say over it,
'I'll never see that one again.'
If you want to explain eternity,
you had better use negative terms:
'I'll never see. I'll never come back.'

So what's the good of sunning yourself? to be
a sadness, roasted and beautiful, an enticing scent?

When we left the seashore, we didn't look at the water
but near the new road we saw a deep pit
and beside it a huge wooden spool wound with heavy cable:
all the conversations of the future, all the silences.

Translated by Chana Bloch and Stephen Mitchell.

FLEUR ADCOCK

The Wars

When they were having the Gulf War
I went to the 18th century.
I could see no glory in this life.

Awake half the night with the World Service,
then off on an early train for news –
secrets, discoveries, public knowledge

lurking on microfilm or parchment:
'I bequeath to my said daughter Mary Adcock
my Bedd and Bedding my oak Clothes Chest and Drawers

my Dressing Table and Looking Glass my Arm chair
my Clock standing in my said Dwelling house,
And one half part or share of all my Pewter.'

When it was over and not over,
and they offered us the Recession instead,
I went back further, pursuing the St Johns,

the Hampdens, the Wentworths to their deathbeds:
'Item I give to my wives sonne . . .'
(Ah, so she *had* been married before!)

'. . . Mr Edward Russell fiftie pounds,
and to John his brother ten pounds by the yeare
to be paid him soe long as he followes the warrs . . .'

KATERINA ANGHELAKI-ROOKE

Spring Offering for Yanoussa
YANOUSSA COUNTS HER POSSESSIONS

Do I look better in the light or in the dark?

Nature slowly grows old and worn
Before the eyes of the woman
Sitting motionless on a chair
Like a raindrop on a leaf.

Yanoussa has reached that point
Where nothing advances
And nothing is instantaneous.
She's inside it all and everywhere without;
Everything feeds her and she's no longer fed.
Who has gone? Who is to come? Silence.

So she counts. A garden.
Beyond the trees the school
And then the sea.
Then there's the dog. A relative.
The days pass. She earns no money.

Today the earth drinks and drinks.
A good shower.
She considers the burgeoning shoots
And the branches bending beneath the weight
And how much longer she'll be witness to it all.
Forty-nine and the obsession over.

YANOUSSA AND THE NON-APPARENT

Would it have been revealed had I not suffered?

Stones and grasses,
Things and sunset canopies
With a crimson death,
Emerge from their silence.
Not that they speak –
For that would be contrary to their nature –
But they embody the truth of the woman
For they reveal their own to her.
The sea has another face –
The rock,
The blackbird the branch,
The force of the flower
Mud.
The power of dark life
Bursts into stigmas and stamens,
Into frantic gasps like those
That once enslaved you.
Now down, down below, can you smell?
Can you smell the flow of the non-apparent?

Translated by the author and Jackie Willcox.

SIMON ARMITAGE

Becoming Of Age

The year the institutions would not hold.
The autumn when the convicts took their leave.
The month the radio went haywire, gargled
through the long-range forecast, and their names.

The fortnight of the curfew, and the cheese-wire
of the Klaxon slicing day from night, night
from day. The clear, unclouded ocean

of the sky. The week we met. The afternoon
we might have seen a ghost, a scarecrow
striding boldly down The Great North Road
towards us, wearing everything he owned.

The minute in the 'phone box with the coin,
the dialling tone, the disagreement – heads
to leave him be, to let him go to ground
and keep the public footpaths trodden down,
the green lanes and the bridleways, or tails
to turn him in to the authorities.

Then on the glass, each in its own time – one,
two, three, four, five, six fingerprints of rain.

Ice

As if the window that will not close
and the bath water being barely hot enough
and the wet towels
were not enough to worry over.

But your favourite dress
is damp and unironed;
you haven't a stitch to wear
and I am to blame.

Now you will turn the house inside out.
Now you will tear through the wardrobe –
more shoes than Mrs Marcos, hangers
relieved of their shirts and blouses

till the armchair is constricted
with fabrics and colours
and the carpet alive
with cuffs, sleeves and collars.

I wait outside
by the fractured pipe
on the gable end
as the cream of your bath water

finds its way along the street
and turns the corner.
Already its edges
are beginning to harden.

PATRICIA BEER

Senior Members

Senior members, writing
To the college chronicle
Give more news than they mean to.
With only one name on show
The class of '17 must all
Have lost men in the fighting.

They deny they are housebound
Yet one speaks of nothing but
A dome she sees in the sun
From her west window, and one
Mentions three years running that
She is very nearly blind.

The class of '84 teach,
Do social work and teach. They
Win lacklustre prizes yet
In God's good time will fan out
Into sinners and saints. We
Shall not know how far they stretch.

The class of '40, my class,
Tell us (I do not write in)
They have retired but conceal
From what. Some of them reveal
How grand their husbands have been.
What odd matters they confess:

One does not use her title
Much – what *was* it? – nowadays.
One has been given a set
Of handbells. One is a hermit.
One appeared on Songs of Praise.
One has moved down to Cornwall.

But grandmothers they all are.
Children they did not conceive,
Nor could have, identify
Them like Saturn's rings. Their sky
Dims but those they are proud of
Skip round them in the night air.

CONNIE BENSLEY

Jump

They were given the bedroom
with the three dolls' houses.

She thought that he, being an analyst,
would involve her in symbolic play,

moving the doll figures about:
'Why have you put the child in the attic?'

*'Why is the mother doll lying
under the table?'* – that sort of thing.

Not at all. He simply kicked off his shoes,
flopped on his bed and went to sleep.

She pulled out the doll from under the table
and put her on the windowsill.

'Jump!' she whispered, *'It's your big chance'*.

ATTILIO BERTOLUCCI

For B . . .

Those little paper planes you make
to send skimming through the twilight
go out like moths on the darkening air
past seeing, and do not return.

So it is with our days, although the night
that will welcome them is less mild
than that of this valley – of fallen leaves,
of silent autumn waters;

and your frail ships, now setting down
dew-buckled, faltering wings.

February Wind

Embittered warlord,
blue-eyed and hard-hearted,
silent and alone in the court of the old winter,
like one waiting with an empty mind,

You can smile – a too-mild January
goes its half-asleep, mournful way,
while February even now stands by
to clot skies, scatter violets on graves.

Mount your horse,
put your horn to your lips.
The hard and empty roads converge
on skylines as blue as your eyes.

Translated by Peter Rafferty.

From: *La Capanna Indiana*

ALAN BROWNJOHN

Barto

Beyond the door the green arrow pointed at
Was one of the dankest human corridors:
Cold, short: one lightbulb swinging unshaded
In a draught from an unseen direction;
No telling what was paint and what was stain:
No guessing what might be roped up inside
The scruffy baskets pushed into that alcove,
Or what the liquid spilt from them might be;
A half-world not to stand mesmerised in,
But no going back to the door of entry
And the first warm place.

                 There is another door,
Leading out to sounds which might be traffic
Or might be the sea at the foot of a cliff,
And that is where the draught is coming from,
An invitation to an ultimate cold . . .
I comb my hair, make sure my back is straight,
And press the tired flesh of my face to smile
As I do not Push Bar to open.

ANDREA CAPES

So Much A Stem

So much a stem. An arm and a leg, they joke,
kiss, go to find a vase tall enough, split
the stems in anticipation of such thirst
in the days to come, musk and ginger pouncing
on each breath.
                        Posed slouch, then an angle goes
humpback, pollen rolls to the floor, rust,
to be left where it lies. Here are foxed paper
and plaster the rain comes through. But no one
will say, Throw them out, just yet.
                                In that silence
fruit goes hard enough to play the kings' old game,
court, rules and racquets warped as in
a convex mirror. Flesh will take the skin
down with it beyond rescue, loaves feed halos
and epitaphs of mould. These people are tidy otherwise.

DAVID DABYDEEN

from *Turner* ('Slaves Thrown Overboard', 1830s)

The sea has brought me tribute from many lands,
Chests of silver, barrels of tobacco, sugar-loaves.
Swords with gleaming handles, crucifixes set in pearls
Which marvelled at, but with the years grown rusty
And mouldy, abandoned – cheap and counterfeit goods:
The sea has mocked and beggared me for centuries,
Except for scrolls in different letterings
Which, before they dissolve I decipher
As best I can. These, and the babbling
Of dying sailors are my means to languages
And the wisdom of other tribes. Now the sea
Has delivered a child sought from the moon in years
Of courtship, when only the light from that silent
Full eye saw me whilst many ships passed by
Indifferently. She hides behind a veil
Like the brides of our village but watches me
In loneliness and grief for that vast space
That still carries my whisper to her ears,
Vaster than the circumference of the sea
That so swiftly drowned my early cries
In its unending roar. There is no land
In sight, no voice carries from that land,
My mother does not answer, I cannot hear her
Calling, as she did when I dragged myself
To the bank of the pond, my head a pool
And fountain of blood, and she runs to me
Screaming, plucks me up with huge hands,
Lays me down on land, as the sea promised
In earlier days, clasped and pitched me sideways
In the direction of our village, my dazed mind
Thought, across a distance big beyond even
The grasp of Salvador (he scribbles numbers
In his book, face wrinkled in concentration
Like an old seal's mouth brooding in crevices

13

Of ice; like my father counting beads
At the end of each day, reckoning
Which calf was left abandoned in the savannah,
Lost from the herd, eaten by wild beasts.
He checks that we are parcelled in equal
Lots, men divided from women, chained in fours
Children substracted from mothers. When all things tally
He snaps the book shut, his creased mouth
Unfolding in a smile, as when, entering
His cabin, mind heavy with care, breeding
And multiplying percentages, he beholds
A boy dishevelled on his bed). For months
It seemed to speed me to a spot where my mother
Waited, wringing her hands, until I woke to find
Only sea. Months became years and I forgot
The face of my mother, the plaid cloth
Tied around her head, the scars on her forehead,
The silver nose-ring which I tugged, made her start,
Nearly rolling me from her lap but catching me
In time, and when I cried out in panic
Of falling, pinned me tightly, always,
To her bosom. Now I am loosed
Into the sea, treading water. I no longer
Call, I have even forgotten the words.
Only the moon remains, watchful and loving
Across a vast space, woman I whisper to,
Companion of my darkest nights.

FRED D'AGUIAR

Inner City

The way a man lets his dog
strip the bark off a young tree
and the children of that man
break branch after branch
till the naked trunk of the thing
stands, a bare stump . . .

Who's to knock their heads together
now that the bobby on the beat
is part of the gang you meet at night
roaming the city's streets,
brazen in his uniform,
smiling through clenched teeth?

That same dog has slipped its leash
stripping a child's flesh
off her soft bones. Who can stop it?
Here's the police just when needed.
They tie a rope around its neck
(the dog's) cutting its steamy breath.

The children report the attack
as something miraculous. One says
he heard the girl's bones crack.
Another liked how the dog wagged
throughout. A third bragged
that after a while it was hard

to tell the colour of the ground
from the girl's smooth brown:
both were dug-up, both were raw;
both were under English law.
The children grow up feeling like dogs
they worship stumps for gods.

PAUL DE ROUX

The Stream

You wait and nothing comes. The days pass.
In each, a certain moment scrapes bottom
– though this isn't it, just a coarse cloth
pulled over the eyes, a state
without real feeling or solidity.
What moves is cloud, and a fringe of blue
appears and promptly disappears, yet
revives something in you for an instant:
and it isn't negligible, this fitful light,
a candle-end you'd shelter
with both arms, a taper to go out with
and confront the high walls
– where a door might open and you'd hear
the light noise of the stream
running between long grass and stones:
the rampart would cast its shadow still,
but there and then you'd be among
earth-smells and the scufflings
of birds, flirting from branch to branch
or skimming water – the water
where you go down now, stripped naked,
and in a shiver clothe yourself
with a new skin the instant of crossing.

Aridity

Seven hundred kilometres from here
a friend writes to say the trees are in flower
– words like a splinter in the flesh.
Here the head nods on a wet grey morning,
flattened, cropped of light.
A depressing desire for sleep
when you know you have to dig
your arid field, so recalcitrant

this morning that the pick
keeps slipping from your swollen hands
and falls derisively
on the cement floor, where it rings and rings:
the real prattle of a daydream.

Translated by Stephen Romer.

PETER DIDSBURY

The Tar On The Roads

Seventh day of the heat wave.
Buying fags after work I tried to remember
the last time the tar on the roads had melted.
She said with cars going past all afternoon
it had sounded as if it were raining.

There was quite a queue at the bus stop.
The man standing next to me said it needed a shelter.
Before the winter came.
I said I knew what a very grim place it was
to find oneself on a January evening.

When the bus arrived, I paid and went upstairs.
All one side was old people, coming back from the coast.
They looked really done in.
They sat alone on the outside of their seats,
and guarded the empty spaces next to them.
It meant I couldn't get myself by a window
on the left of the bus, as I like to,
and consequently had to sit down on the right.

I was faintly annoyed.
And desperately hot.
And rather keenly looking forward
to discussing the heat with my wife,

to telling her all about loudly hissing tar.
As far as I recall,
no-one spoke in that upper saloon
during the whole half-hour of my journey.
I stared from my window.
I watched someone close a window against a draught.
I looked at the yellow fields of the valley floor,
and once I let myself glance across the aisle
at the faces of the pensioners,
but they seemed so tired and angry
that I chose not to do so again.

I was glad when the time came to walk.

The pavements were empty
and the melting road had been dusted with fine white gravel
so that everything looked like a postcard of nineteen-thirteen.

I was very hot indeed.

The worst thing I ever heard on that bus
came out of the mouth of a soldier going on leave
from the Army Transport School,
a mouth he was using to tell another squaddie
of what he'd always wanted to do to old women,
pointing one out down below as we crawled in the traffic,
walking beside us with some letters in her hand.

That was on a summer afternoon too,
one not as hot as this, and when I finally got in the house
the living room was like an oven, and my wife and I turned
each a gasping visage upon the other.
The television was going
and the newsreader was saying to several million people
that Highways Departments throughout the entire region
had been forced to grit the roads today to stop
the tar on them melting, except she didn't call it tar,
having had her orders to refer to it as bitumen.

MAURA DOOLEY

Does It Go Like This?

The day seawater swilled my lungs
he guided me back without ever once touching me.
Lying on shingle, like the two halves
of the equator, I thought my heart would burst,

not knowing in which element it drowned.
Now, two hundred miles from him, beached
on larkspur, lark song, I struggle to remember
something I used to know: *did it go like this? Like that?*

How did it start? At Capel-y-Ffin what rises
from dark red dirt, what's netted now is Heartsease,
flotsam of sheepskull filleted by lice,
a dead pony's ribs taut as ship's rigging

and here, where a draught of summer
rinses tired skin with cuckoo syncopation,
with percussion of bees, old fears rush in
fierce as a tide, blood, not birdsong

pulses at my ear: the strong cross-currents
that beat in these shallows, the meat
and bone under bright meadow grasses,
the heart's tricky business of staying alive.

Remember the day we saw divers trawl the Thames
heavy with rosaries of gas and rope,
angels with black rubber wings and serious faces
dropping through mist and into the deep, like psalms?

What is that tune whose words I try to catch
Does it go like this? Like this? How does it begin?
I dredge up only the middle, a jaded chorus,
of a song I used to know right through by heart.

ALISTAIR ELLIOT

MCMVI

in Memoriam James Adam Elliot, MD ChB (Edinburgh)
Glencoul, August 1901 – Clatterbridge, August 1991

The postman used to shout across the loch
till they rowed over. Once it was for Will,
from Carnegie. 'He's somewhere on the hill
getting our dinner. Who's this Carnegie?' 'Rich.'

Will was fifteen, the eldest, trying to teach
my father (five) his letters. In Glencoul
their lonely house was technically a school.
Their textbook might have been the Pentateuch.

Carnegie offered a fiver and a bookcase
for the School Library. So when Will came back
with the pony, the muzzle-loader and a carcase,
the boys composed a letter. They sent the cheque
to a bookshop, with two clippings from the *Herald*:
Everyman's Library Classics a Shilling Each,
and someone's Hundred Best Books of the World.
They'd fetch them in the boat, from Kyle, next week.

The boys have disappeared: the teacher, Will,
in France, of the same plague as Pericles;
my namesake died when No-Man threw a shell;
my father, of Medea's skin disease.

The books may well survive. The one I'd like,
perhaps on a tray in the rain now, marked '10 p',
is *Vanity Fair*, in which the boy got stuck
half up the tree of knowledge. I would look
for the words he read, to everybody's glee,
'He was a man of charming gravy-tea.'

ROY FISHER

Photographers' Flowers

When old men get well-known again
and interviews come to the cottages,
the *dachas*, the garden corners,

there are pictures taken away:
well-known old men. Daylight
from the side and the hard old head
thinking about daylight. Silver
stubble, hands let still.

There's a secret that keeps them going.
Each has beside him at all
times, in a wineglass
or a scrubbed-out fishpaste jar,
his flower. That's how they live,
quietly seated, each with his dried
seed head or spirited weed.

So the photographers say;
searching the dresser for a glass,
the yard for a flower.

Stop

Spent all his life
playing for time.
All of it.

ANNIE FOSTER

Harebell In The Beck

On the palm of my hand sits the end of summer harebell,
a skinny tendril of green with a five point star to cup the bell.
The petal, blown, all of a piece, shows its vein.
I don't want to hold it until the warmth makes it droop
so I trail the stem in the numb water of the beck,
the frame collapses and I let it go,
a spot of sky against the slaty beck bottom.

I think of the slender premise on which all my loves are
    leaning
and how I try time and time over to let go
those who are poised to leave and those
whom the water has already taken away.

JOHN GREENING

Katie In A Prospect of D.C.

Outside the Oval Office,
my daughter started
to sing Humpty Dumpty.

Then, at a rising black wall
that dropped to a V,
she stopped singing and cried

for a flag of stars
to wave past the dark
windows of the Space Museum.

On Capitol Hill, she
chattered towards a life-
size image of Jesus,

was silent before the statue
of the Father of Television,
heard the floor whisper.

But approaching Watergate,
she pressed her investigative nose
to the glass, and broke in

on our conversations again
and again to report
what all the king's men couldn't.

IAN HAMILTON

Work in Progress

A six foot three American breathologist
Has cornered me for cocktails: 'Suck on these'
He says, and chucks me a slim vol.
Entitled: *Big*. Two words a line, at most,
Nine lines a page, typography incurably diseased,
It's signed: 'To Ian, in pulse-harmony –
You dig? Love, Irv. November, seventy-three.'
And on the sleeve, his photograph:
He's felling trees.

JOHN HARTLEY WILLIAMS

Das Doppelgehen

(i)
In that life the cobblestones
shone with rain, & the trams

came clicking with faces
behind the streaked-up panes

in which we rode, thinking
of rooves that shd have kept out the wet,

the steel above our heads,
the statue in the park on the island

in the river that was a hotel,
where the senior members of our race met

& I sat mixing ink with wine
describing political exhaustion

so brilliantly
you fell in love with me at once.

(ii)
They were more like us
than we were.

Nothing moved in their symphony orchestras
when they played *The Rite of Spring*.

No fiddlers threw scarves over their shoulders
& left with a toss of the head.

No percussionists
waited for years to say: 'Chin chin!'

And the conductor was a proud man.
You cd tell that by the way he shrank

ever so slowly into his socks during
the non-performance of the piece

we'd written that morning on a bench
under the dripping boughs of a tree

we'd seen in a film
of amoral events

viewed thru
a mud-splashed windscreen.

That was us.
In a taxi.

Bouncing down unmade streets
to the end of town,

a *dacha* in a fruit orchard
& a man in shirt sleeves, waiting . . .

(iii)
'There I am!' you said.
He was tending his garden,

hammering nails into the water
which had so increased his stock of pools.

When people discover life is perfect –
there they are.

They fall into a blue drowse.
They smile.

How affably he showed us the way,
 when we climbed the stairs to bed that evening

& the wind blew in like a radio
& it was just warm enough to be cold!

We felt the blood surge in us like rain
& our mouths wd have met like that, over & over,

if the door had not banged open
& he not stood there, petrified,

moving his lips
without a sound . . .

(iv)
We stopped kissing, laughed
& invited him in

& gave him Schnapps, & he watched
the cool swoop of yr bodice below yr neck

& yr pale skin sinking
below the horizon

down into that shadow life
over the lip of tall buildings,

a narrow cleft, falling & floating,
into an imaginary bliss

while we waited patiently
for him to tell his joke & go.

SEAMUS HEANEY

The Gravel Walks

1.
River gravel. In the beginning, that.
High summer, and the angler's motorbike
Deep in roadside flowers, like a fallen knight
Whose ghost we'd lately questioned: 'Any luck?'

As the engines of the world prepared, green nuts
Kept hanging their cheeks closer to the whirlpool.
The trees dipped down. The flints and sandstone-bits
Worked themselves smooth and smaller in a sparkle

Of shallow, hurrying, barley-sugar water
Where minnows schooled and bare-assed children bathed –
An eternity that ended once a tractor
Dropped its link-box in the riverbed

And cement mixers began to come to life,
And men in dungarees, like sunstruck shades,
Mixed concrete, loaded, wheeled, turned, wheeled, as if
The Pharaoh's brickyards burned inside their heads.

2.
Hoard and praise the verity of gravel.
Gems for the undeluded. Milt of earth.
Its plain, champing song against the shovel
Soundtests and sandblasts words like 'honest worth'.

Beautiful in or out of the river,
The kingdom of gravel was inside you too –
Deep down, far back, clear water running over
Pebbles of carmel, hailstone, mackerel-blue.

But the actual washed stuff kept you slow and steady
As you went stooping with your barrow full
Into an absolution of the body,
The shriven life your bones and marrow feel.

So walk on air against your better judgement,
Establishing real presence in between
The solid batches mixed with grey cement
And a tune called 'The Gravel Walks' that conjures green.

DIANA HENDRY

All Hail the Hollyhocks

Freaks, flapping their leaves
like albatross wings when
to be discreet they should lean
against some husbanding wall,
pose prettily beside a door.

Exposed and unsupported
these show-offs flaunt their flowers
in public. Neat, low clumps
of things mumble at their feet,
the clingers and grippers,
the rooters and spreaders
who talk of decorum.

The hussies ignore them, intent
on the terrible toil of growing,
the doubtful strength,
the engorged bud,
the threat of snail slime, rust and slug
and the shame
of being too tall, too much,
too altogether hollyhock.

Well, now they're wind instruments
flowering at every stop.
They're summer's gothic,
they're hitting the high spots,
they're shooting their mouths off
hysterical to have made it
past the clothes-line
past the first floor windows.

Gangling, tranced teenagers with earphones on,
they're humming sun and sky,
beyond everything,
shaking with laughter.
Tomorrow they'll flash another flower or two

bewitching, true.

SELIMA HILL

Much Against Everyone's Advice

Much against everyone's advice,
I have decided I must not be put off any longer
from coming into your room
and telling you the truth, as best I can.
There's something I've got to tell you I will say.
Yes, I have been practising, you see –
you would be proud of me.
Alone in this ridiculous café,
with stiffened hair,
holding your last letter
like a penitent teenager
stranded on a cliff
who clutches the Bible
thank God she remembered to bring,
I have been practising.

Can you still see the boat
that dropped from the sky
right into Granny's garden,
just as two little girls,
never to visit fairyland again,

strayed out of the hydrangea bed?
And Granny turned over in her sleep
and saw a blonde young pilot
who looked like Jesus
gazing into her eyes
from just about the level of her bedroom window?
Who ran his hands backwards and forwards
along his glossy cockpit
as if it were a prize bull
and not a stunted machine
that had ruined our lives for ever;
who looked down at the boat
as if she were a dancer, in perfect order,
and not a boat
creaking among squashed roses in our border?

All year he had been practising for this,
and I have too.
Much against everyone's advice,
I have decided to tell you everything,
poor worm.

The Freezer-Tunnel

Yes, it's a freezer-tunnel!

Say goodbye to the pinks,
and the tall fox-gloves,
and the soft-pawed cat
that hunts in the field of sheep;

to delicate sentiments
such as placing flowers
on the tomb of a complete stranger;

to beautiful drawings
found over a long period of time
through searches of the archives
of Swiss mental institutions;

to bees, and important operations
in bee-management;

to the singer who, just as you thought
she was failing, would float
some absolutely ravishing high note;

to the poodle whose owner
carefully lifts her up
as he too avoids the jellyfish
that's lolling on the beach;

to threshing;
to pig-snouts covered in flies;

and approach it
as an abseiler would,
or an industrial abseiler,
who scales glass:

approach it with your best concentration.

MICHAEL HOFMANN

The Out-of-Power

I walked on New Year's Eve from Trotsky's house
under the lindens, banana and rubber trees
of the Calle Viena – the jerried watchtowers,
the outside windows all bricked up or half-bricked in,
and the place where the crazed muralist Siqueiros
had sprayed the walls with automatic fire and still missed –

to the house of ex-President de la Madrid,
just two weeks out of office, and a reduced
ex-presidential complement of three guards on the
    pavement –
a glimpse down the drive to parked imported cars,
the pool, flowering shrubs, *frou-frou*, rhubarb,
glass in the windows, ice clinking in the glasses.

Guanajuato Two Times

I could keep returning to the same few places
till I turned blue; till I turned into
José José
on the sleeve of his new record album
'What is Love?';
wearing a pleasant frown and predistressed denims;
reading the double-page spread ('The Trouble with José
José')
on his drink problem,
comparing his picture 'Before' and 'After' . . .
I could slowly become a ghost, slowly familiar,
slowly invisible, amiable, obtuse . . .
I could say 'Remember me?' to the blank bellhop,
and myself remember
the septet in the bandstand playing 'Winchester Cathedral',
and the clown coming in for coffee
and to count his takings and take off his face . . .
I could take on all my former beds for size.
Meander knowingly through twelve towns with twelve street
names between them.
Sit on both sides of the municipal kissing seats,
shaking my head at the blanket men
and the hammock men, in their humorous desperation
offering me hammocks for four, for five, for six . . .
I could learn the Spanish for
'I shall have returned' or 'Hullo, it's me again!'
and get the hang of the double handshake,
first the palms, then the locked thumbs.
My dreams would moulder and swell and hang off me
like pawpaws. I could stand and sway like a palm,
or rooted like a campanile, crumbling slightly
each time the bells tolled, not real bells
but recordings of former bells,
and never for me.

Gottfried Benn: Chopin

Not much of a conversationalist,
ideas weren't his strong suit,
ideas miss the point,
when Delacroix expounded his theories
it made him nervous, he for his part
could offer no explanation of the Nocturnes.

A poor lover;
mere shadow in Nohant
where George Sand's children
rejected his attempts
at discipline.

His tuberculosis
took the chronic form,
with repeated bleeding and scarring;
a creeping death,
as opposed to one
in convulsions of agony
or by firing squad:
the piano (Erard) was pushed back against the door
and Delphine Potocka
sang to him
a violet song in his last hour.

He took three pianos with him to England:
Pleyel, Erard, Broadwood,
for twenty guineas
he would give fifteen-minute recitals in the evenings
at the Rothschilds' and the Wellingtons', in Strafford House
to the assembled cummerbunds;
then, dark with fatigue and imminent death,
he went home
to the Square d'Orléans.

Then he burned his sketches
and manuscripts,
didn't want any leftover scraps
betraying him –
at the end he said:
'I have taken my experiment
as far as it was possible for me to go.'

Each finger was to play
to no more than its natural strength,
the fourth being the weakest
(twinned with the middle finger).
At the start, they occupied the keys
of E, F sharp, G sharp, B and C.

Anyone hearing
certain of his Preludes
in country seats or
at altitude,
through open French windows
on the terrace, say, of a sanatorium,
will not easily forget it.

He composed no operas,
no symphonies,
only those tragic progressions
from artistic conviction
and with a small hand.

By Gottfried Benn (1886–1956)

Translated by Michael Hofmann

TED HUGHES

Laws of the Game

She had too much so with a smile you took some.
Of everything she had you had
Absolutely nothing, so you took some.
At first, just a little.

Still she had so much she made you feel
Your vacuum, which nature abhorred,
So you took your fill, for nature's sake.
Because her great luck made you feel unlucky
You had redressed the balance, which meant
Now you had some too, for yourself.
As seemed only fair. Still her ambition
Claimed the natural right to screw you up
Like a crossed-out page, tossed into a basket.
Somebody, on behalf of the gods,
Had to correct that hubris.
A little touch of hatred steadied the nerves.

Everything she had won, the happiness of it,
You collected
As your compensation
For having lost. Which left her absolutely
Nothing. Even her life was
Trapped in the heap you took. She had nothing.
Too late you saw what had happened.
It made no difference that she was dead.
Now that you had all she had ever had
You had much too much.
                         Only you
Saw her smile as she took some.
At first, just a little.

ALAN JENKINS

Jellyfish

We'd hired the car 'to take a skite around' –
turfstacks, marram, the scrotumtightening sea.
You had just explained how you could rhyme
silicon and *silicone*, since both are found
in a *pebble of quartz* – etymologically –

when Warren Zevon sang out from the stereo,
'If Cali–fornia slides in–to the O–cean,
like the mystics and statistics say it will . . .'
and I saw the West Coast, in slow motion,
sheer off and slip underwater, and,

a million or so years after that, some
gentle creature slope out of soupy slime
where we'd parked the car and walked the strand,
then peer at a shoal of un-biodegradable
silicone implants flopped on the sand –

no more apt to scry how far they'd come
from their origins, or guess the stir
they'd once caused in the human breast, than we
to scrutinize a score of beached jellyfish that stared
up at us, and stared, and stared, and stared.

ROBERT JOHNSTONE

Pirrie

Imagine a daguerreotype of me in my birthday suit
sprawled on a polar bearskin rug.

That's the snow of winters in Canada
where Mother was widowed when I was two.

Eliza Swann, from County Antrim,
she married the son of a sea-captain there.

Imagine me riding a swan's back
away from the marble face of my father.

That was us crossing the Atlantic,
the Captain our pilot when our ship came in.

The forest reborn on the town quays
was the whole world visiting Belfast.

I was fifteen years old when I entered the shipyard.
I got my hands dirty learning the business.

I never grew up, I was small my whole life.
I backed my cheques with inexhaustible charm.

With my knife I could pick a skelf of metal
out of the white of a fellow's eye.

My hands are tiny, you see, like a child's;
they never slipped once – I was famous for it.

Imagine me surfing the bow wave
of the grandest ship in the biggest fleet.

That was me repping for Harland,
crisscrossing the great circles,

convinced that numbers explain it all –
I could run a country with a column of numbers.

I seem to be melting into whiteness,
an image in silver that hasn't been fixed,

a white-haired old man invisible against
the tiles of my dairy, my hospital wards.

I've a submarine room in the grounds here,
a glass dome under one of the lakes.

I know if I went there I'd see my own death,
a snowstorm of pages despite the gloom,

a mountain of snow looming from blackness,
a polar bear waking and rolling over.

Words are fading off the pages
of even Mother's book of advice.

A foamy scum is whitening even
the black sleech of the Lagan banks,

where some wag sculpted a snowman of me
smaller than life, with glowter eyes.

Behind the staging's an iceberg of marble,
my men are a frieze in low relief,

shipwrights, welders, boilermakers, apprentices,
all the dead down the sides of my monument.

JAAN KAPLINSKI

The sun shines on the red wall and the wall is warm.
I feel it with my hand, I put my cheek against it.
Nevertheless, I feel there is something between us,
something that keeps me far from the real wall,
from the red colour and the sun. There is something
that keeps me in Plato's world of ideas
until my blood begins to throb and the sun sets,
the red wall turns black and cold in the darkness
and crocuses under my window wither.
Transcience engraves new inscriptions into my self
as if I were an old churchbell. The voice
grows clearer and clearer and is heard farther than ever
over walls, over throbbing blood, over the world of ideas
and from beyond its borders a blowing wind
carries the saffron aroma of black crocuses.

It gets cold in the evening. The sky clears.
The wind dies out, and the smoke
rises straight up. The flowering maple
no longer buzzes. A carp
plops in the pond. An owl hoots twice
in its nest in the ash tree.
The children are asleep. On the stairs,
a long row of shoes and rubber boots.
It happened near Viljandi: an imbecile boy
poured gasoline on the neighbour's three-year-old son
and set him on fire. I ran for milk.
You could see the yellow maple from far off
between the birches and the spruce. The evening star
was shining above the storehouse. The boy survived,
probably maimed for life. The night will bring frost.
Plentiful dew.

Translated by the author with Sam Hamill & Riina Tamm.

41

ALEKSANDR KUSHNER

Someone's crying all night.
Just behind the wall someone's crying.
    If I could, I would try
to help, but the aggrieved won't invite me.

    It's stopped. No, there it is.
'Go to sleep,' you say. 'Sleep; you imagined . . .'
    I need rest, I need rest.
In the dark, though, my heart's contracted.

    People crying these days?
Where'd you hear any crying, I wonder.
    No age kept dryer eyes
than ours, raised under a tearless banner.

    Maybe children – but they,
hearing, 'Shame on you!' will fall silent.
    So in darkness we lie;
only the watch on the table's unquiet.

    Someone's crying nearby.
'Sleep,' you tell me again; 'I don't hear it.'
    If I asked, your reply
would give rain on the roof as your theory.

    It's stopped. Now it starts up,
as if there's still more, deeper grief, hiding.
    But I'm falling asleep.
'Wake up! Listen!' you say. 'Someone's crying.'

Palace

Here are armchairs in which no one has ever sat,
here are sofas where no one relaxed;
at this desk no one dealt with affairs of state,
handled the miniature obelisk of malachite,
or kept papers in the decorative box.
This magnificent canopy never hung
the anchoring weight of its tassels above
the eyes of anyone
gazing up at its chartreuse and lilac surf;
this is Rome, and Greece, and Paris, arranged
in a whimsical, capricious blend of motifs;
semicircular niches running in a chain;
passages, galleries, columns, and suites;
this is Brenna – moulded, patterned, and carpeted
in emerald, violet, whiter than chalk –
squeezing Cameron's beginning out of sight;
Voronikhin continued Brenna's unfinished work
– it's too much.
                    The capacity of the soul,
so it seems, is too small to endure all this.
As the darkness falls
and footsteps die out, objects' gazes fix
on each other: vases, mirrors, candlesticks.
Over here, in the corner, cloudlike, a plaster god;
there, at home on its table, a lamp has trod
on a pattern traced out entirely in gold
and looks irremovable, as if joined by a weld.
Everything has a particular property – a gleam
or a mist, an allusion to its volume and length.
It's not objects I love, but their link
with the world we live in, into which they come.
If we ever were able to figure out
their patterns, patterns we don't yet understand,
which are powerful, since our eyes are caught
– perhaps we'd be happier after that,
closer to a secret that darkness has screened.

These are halls for phantoms to haunt; this can
almost be called an Italian villa; a paradise
lost, flooded by rain,
covered with snow, so that no one ever walks in
without whispering to his remaining life, 'Goodbye!'
This Elysium was made by man with the goal
of betraying confusion in our gaze
as we pass through the rooms like geese, in single file;
in this bedroom, none has lain on this gauzy pink haze.
But the masters of this heaven on earth,
of chandeliers like the sun, of chalices full of stars,
really lived lower – in the right-hand wing, as I've heard.
Gilded objects, or waxed – all a material mirage!
And yet once, amid these marble dreams, I was kissed,
surreptitiously, on the run; we strayed
through these halls till we'd missed
the prescribed path. When I die, my last wish
will be finding that crossing, that very square of parquet.

This wonder on a backdrop of January snow;
Aphrodite, Eros, sculpted clusters of grapes;
the evident swoon that the matted eyeballs show;
a mélange of every flowering, bounty, and age;
and beyond plate-glass windows, the whirl of flakes;
these white muses who went on such a long walk
that a snowstorm covered up the road home;
this dry-as-a-rash, icy milk;
the chill-blue protection that glass becomes . . .
Here there's as much daring and risk, here I find
as much longing and craziness (whichever you prefer),
as in life, which waits, rubbing its temples outside,
whether I do remember and miss her
who has vanished . . .
                              No, too much done, too many years;
I forgot, and let go my hand. I forgot,

and – well, isn't the snow out the window more sparse?
And besides, no one ever sat in these chairs
or kept any papers in that box.

Translated by Paul Graves and Carol Veland.

Note:
The palace is that of Paul I at Pavlovsk, begun by Charles
Cameron (1730s–1812), a Scottish architect of the neoclassical
style, in 1782–86, and enlarged and remodelled by Vincenzo
Brenna (1745–1820) in the 1790s. After a fire in 1803, it was
redone by the Russian architect Andrei Voronikhin (1759–1814).

DOUGLAS LIVINGSTONE

A Darwinian Preface

The crab, the clot, the muzzle or the knife:
patiently, the nocturnal terrorisms
stalk. Even the brave know hardly of rest,
aware a body's little but a glove
stretched from metatarsals to neocortex
on a stiffening frame. A hand as strange
clenches on coiled lengths of fear: that old vortex
steeled by the usual mundane heroisms.
Your heart wins armour from confronting life,
yet stays unlatched, anticipating love.
Each dawn claims thanks and welcome, and gets blessed.
Perhaps the sea indeed did suckle you
through all its prisms, its diurnal range.
There is no help for it. Best buckle to.

MICHAEL LONGLEY

Remembrance Day
after Ida Gerhardt

The names of the fallen,
names we forgot so soon,
are sometimes lamented
by the howling stormwind.

Put your ear to the poles.

That din overwhelmed me
below Zalk and Veecaten –
too much for poles to bear
almost, and metal wires.

Polderland
after Hendrik Marsman

I walk through the polders
beneath infernal showers,
a landscape without end,
without end the roadways

that reach the horizon;
against banks of darkness
the watery moonlight
daubs heaven's backdrop.

O land of thirty streams,
benighted sects have split
hairs about God, Mammon,
power, the crown of thorns.

A landscape without end,
without end the roadways
that reach the horizon;
I walk towards morning
in watery moonlight.

The Water-Lily
after Frederik van Eeden

I love the white water-lily, immaculate,
Unfolding her corolla in daylight.

Rising from the cold sediments of the lake
She has seen the light and then unlocked

Her heart of gold: on the surface at one
With herself, her very own creation.

TESSA LUND

From: Poems From The Caves

The small crowd shift and stare
in the cold air underground.

They go over the house,
a primate's grooming,
touch nose and cheekbones
the knotted flints like muscle
cramps in the sandstone;
the aboriginal, gravid stone
and the man in evidence:

Homo sapiens sapiens
the first
to work a cave surface

a sunless journeyman.
The first cutting tooth of his
imagination, a painted, deep
infusion of blood, the blushing of
an old man, blackens and lusts,
livid in the colours of a stone age
that will go on to embrace him
in the tunnel, corpus callosum,
and second chamber of the brain.

Now the two halves can look
at one another, marvelling,
or wander in the very cave itself
among its large beasts.

Here we are, rather late, and tourists
saying when can we go back to our hotels?
Here we are and the sign outside warned us
caves are only a retreat towards the cold.
Our stories are not yet made sure
so no one can let his friends go back
or who will corroborate our version?
Our ears strain towards the guide.
There is no ease in being a tourist,
we have no comfort, but we would not
return empty-handed to our country.
Who then will hear of our discomfort?
When we recount our experiences abroad
who will know at Pech Merle
that we touched a negative hand?

CLARE MACDONALD SHAW

A Waste of Breath

The drinker shields fine wine from an invasive scent.
Palate numb, he scorns a dissolute thirst for oils
pumped from hot wells in flesh, as pores dispense
legal tincture of opium, atomized proof of spirit migrating,
spice-ghost, *spectre de la rose*.

Slow tongues, learning the grammar of taste,
progress from monosyllables of beer, gin, rum,
to fluency in Châteauneuf-du-Pape. Illiterate nostrils
find no primers for scent's dead language –
nouns like otto, attar, root of calamus, and verbs
for smearing necks over the pulse of blood
as incense swung. Passwords to primitive brain
survive: carnation of flesh, narcissus, old narcotic.
Myrrh's that fungal shadow at the heart,
but whose nose can tell styrax from opopanax,
or censor ambergris, floating vomit of whale?

The alchemist has turned designer, setting out phials
among vanishing creams to subvert. He mixes metaphors
of lily and tuberose, translated to aldehyde, adding
chemical similes of musk. Trapped in stoppered glass,
his compounds flaunt their images: odalisques and amazons
spell out bold civet or milk of vanilla.

Dogs, children, fluent in dung and flowers
need no interpreter. Older senses fade with the green wind,
Vent Vert, in a blue hour, preserving dried stems of
                                                    bouquets:
wine thickened year by year in the hymnbook cupboard,
vinegar air sousing wood and word; or a scarf of chypre
round the mother's neck, faint lilac print on moss.

Scholars teach no art of aromatics;
the good cry rape for lavender plucked and stripped.
Though rosemary oils the brain, and nothing so green as
                                        shades
of vetiver will cool the eye, the cynic says: *lilies of the*
                                        field?
– *hydroxycitronellal now, a waste of breath.* Do absolutes
remain,
quintessences, alcohol for the soul? Exorcise small demons
per fumum, burning cypress with sandalwood; keep to the lit
                                        path.

Offer the guest a dry cologne, or vintage frangipani,
rich as oloroso. Scent the bitters of life? Prepare for
                                        disbelievers:
wormwood in vermouth is easier to swallow.

GEORGE MACKAY BROWN

The Bridegroom from the Sea

I stopped at 'The Arctic Whaler'
To give me courage.
Also to hire a horse, Bess, at the yard.

There was that ale-house in Kirbister.
Bess wouldn't pass the door
Till we'd dug our faces deep in the grain.

Aith in Sandwick, what horseman
Could ever resist your malt?
I sat at the fire with four thirsty ploughmen.

I'd deserted *Susie* my yawl that day
To bespeak a bride,
A Birsay lass, well dowered.

I was wearing my best black suit.
At Dounby, didn't I set the moth-balled elbow
In a pool of sour ale?

The deeper that nag bore me
Among the barley fields
The sweeter the sea sang in my ears.

Good reports of that lass –
Bonny, a baker of good bread,
A golden hand in the butter-kirn.

After the shebeen in Marwick
I had to rest in a ditch.
I woke up. Bess was away in a green wind.

I never stood at that bride's door.
I footed it home to Hamnavoe
I said to my boat next morning,

'*Susie*, sweetheart, forgive me.
Our creels never lacked a lobster.
Your thwarts threshed with continuous silver.

Brutish servitude, hooves and millstones.
You and I, *Susie*, will go still
Among the blue-and-silver coursers out west'.

JAMIE MCKENDRICK

Et in Orcadia Ego

Having heard the Orkneys were like Eden
we sold up everything and bought a farm.
A subsistence farm, I called it. There wasn't sun
enough for solar panels – the rays fell
at such an oblique angle, it was clear
they were heading for somewhere else,
some kinder place with trees. All round the year
the big winds tore about with wasteful power.
I felt that just by being there
I was tilting at windmills. Did I have to
build them as well? Since then I've often thought
if we'd run the waterpipes beneath the henshit
like smoky lava on the floor of the coop
we could have had hot water winterlong.

The last straw was a goat-breeding project.
Hoping the meat might sell, I'd bought
this Anglo-Nubian billy to beget
a nation and populate our land. I left him
tethered to a mulberry shrub . . . when God
stumbled upon the body of Abel
in the murderous quiet of the day
and sent Cain off to chew the bitter cud
he must have felt as I felt in that empty place.
The farm pony was looking darkly innocent
and the kid had withdrawn into his yellow gaze
– the colour made me think of Nile mud –
his jaw stove in by the pony's hoof.
All attempts to heal or tend him failed
and, though neither I nor Anne could keep it down,
we ended eating our last chance to stay.

City of Winds

When we threw caution to the winds the city
was the city of winds which blew from the four quarters, the
eight points
of the windrose, a star that creaked and skittered on its hinge
and reared dustdevils – helices, rootless, almost human, (us?) –

and a palm frond swept the public garden paths
like a bird feigning lameness – shuffle, hop, another shuffle –
while a plinth of sunlight turned the sea's roof turquoise
and tides lashed the concrete calthrops of the breakwater.

On a calm day once from Possillipo I saw
the sea, way out, extrude a pillar of salt, a corkscrew
that tapped the deep and lifted shoals to rain down on our
roofs
like wingless birds who'd flown through sheer assumption.

The Vulcanologist

Athanasius Kircher
having completed his
key work on Coptic grammar
(and rightly linked it to the
hieroglyphs) left the cardinals
in Rome and set about his Latin tract
on volcanoes. He visited Etna and Vesuvius
and Vesuvius he entered, let down the inner
walls by lengths of rope, growing smaller and
smaller like a bug on a thread tacked to the sky's
vault with tiny pins of adamant. There he swung past
fumaroles with poison yellow plumes, abseiling through
gardens of brimstone and red cinders. He saw the vestibule
he knew would lead to a vast network of subterranean flames,
lakes of bitumen and burning conduits threading land and ocean
from Iceland to Patagonia. In his book he mapped fire's empire and
its outposts, the whole racked body of Hephaestos, whose molten heart
we build our spindly cities on, and plant and tend our perishable groves.

GLYN MAXWELL

Well Doctor Well

Well you get them headless, legless, fallen
Naked, dressed, undressed by women,
Sometimes nice to stare at, though
More often than not not really, no.
They turn their clothes to cloths, and men
To shapes the cloths are hanging on.
They're heavy, twisted, ugly and still.
If anything stays still, they will.

Dr Who, of course, has them come lop-
Sidedly smashing out of each clothes-shop
Pale deniable thugs of nylon,
Powered by some new hood from hell
And murderous for a single reason.
Though we have them just like that as well.

Shake

Now, get the immigrants' carts off the byway,
kneel and unfurl with your many sisters
the banners as big as the village, and shake
the homes out into the Square. She is coming.

Cordon and number, commence the anthem,
rummage the country for a fitting folkdance
and resurrect it, for now she is coming,
and the sons of the village are smiling on her chances.

Her hair is yellow. Her hair is corn-yellow
as the fields of the Europe we do not remember
from black-and-white pictures snapped in silence
by boy West Virginians stumbling on faces.

Observe her Party do decently somewhere
the wine's recommended, and watch her gracing
each Sunday glossy, a brand new angel
spinning through air in the nineteen-nineties.

ANDREW MOTION

Them and Us and Ovid

When they bowed down –
so we could see the brain-spike sticking out of their skulls
and the birdshit hair we thought had been silver –

when they bowed down
the statues were huge iron-necked toys for children to climb on
and wise political men to make away with.

I climbed on too
and my statue, the wonder I set myself astride,
turned into a stallion which galloped off towards the forest,

hooves clicking up sparks from the flinty earth
so the entire landscape soon seemed on fire
and flowing like a river under the sun –

except there was no sun, nothing to pierce
the forest wall when I broke through at last,
sinking into the beautiful deep silence and darkness

of nothing moving,
where I was lost to the people
I once believed in and wished all the good in the world.

*

I have come to the window
for sweet night air
and a tawny sea
of sunflower faces
all staring after the light.

This is the best:
no future, no past,
only the creak
of the garden cooling,
a bell behind trees,

and right next door
the kiss of your foot
on cold tiles
as you climb out of our bed
to discover where I am now.

When news of my forgiveness came
I'd lived so long in exile that the thought
of having any sort of life to rediscover
seemed a joke. No, more than just a joke –

a sort of crime. I half imagined I had seen a grey volcano-
victim dozing in his ash
rise up, dust off his shirt and trousers,
then get on with business in the world.

Or if not that, at least my sombre statue
trundled back into a square where crowds appeared
and dragged me to my feet: a name again,
one hand held up in blessing or a plea for peace.

I think it never crossed their minds I'd want to stay.
They wouldn't and they still don't understand
that here, in so much time, I've learnt to love the clack
of dialects I still can hardly speak; to love the days

for being mine and mine alone; to love the nights
for showing me how fast the simplest stream
can tunnel through my bones, how easily the air
will blow without a murmur through my open veins.

PAUL MULDOON

The Sonogram

Only a few weeks ago, the sonogram of Jean's womb
resembled nothing so much
as a satellite map of Ireland:

now the image
is so well-defined we can make out not only a hand
but a thumb;

on the road to Spiddal, a woman hitching a ride;
a gladiator in his net, passing judgement on the crowd.

LES MURRAY

The Fellow Human

Beside Anchor Flour school frocks dimmed with redknuckle soaps
poverty's hardly poverty nowadays, here.
The mothers who drive up under tortoiseshell pines to the
    school
are neat in jeans and track tops
and have more self and presence on hand in the car.

Their four-wheeled domains are compound of doors to slam
but only their children do. Drama is private, for home.
Here, the tone is citizenly equal.
The woman with timber-grey braids and two modelled in
    cold-cream
chat through and minutely circle inside their opening wry
    smile.

Another, serene, makes a sad-comic mouth below glasses
for her fine-necked rugby-mad boy, also in glasses,
and registers reed notes in the leatherhead birds' knotty
    music
as they unpick a red-gold judge's wig of bloom
in the silky-oak tree above the school's two classes.

To remodel the countryside, in this post-job age of peace,
women have slept with trucks, raised houses by hammer and
    telephone,
plucked sopping geese and whitened them to stone,
and suddenly most sex writing seems slave-era boasting, in
    the face,
living mousseline, never-shaved, of the fellow human.

The ginger local woman alighting from the saddle of her van
talks to a new friend who balances a baby on one hip
and herself on the other. The two nod upwards, and laugh.
Not for heavy old reasons does the one new here go barefoot
but to be arrived, at home in this dust-warm landscape.

Ultima Ratio

Translated from the German of Friedrich
Georg Jünger (1945).

Like vapour, the titanic scheme
is dissipated,
everything grows rusty now
that they created.

They hoped to make their craze
the lasting Plan,
now it falls apart everywhere,
sheet steel and span.

Raw chaos lies heaped up
on wide display.
Be patient. Even the fag-ends
will crumble away.

Everything they made contained
what brought their fall
and the great burden they were
crushes them all.

JULIE O'CALLAGHAN

Short-Changed

The gals behind the hosiery counter
have looks of despair on their faces.
Is this any way to leave a cash drawer,
with no quarters or dimes or singles?
How the heck are they supposed to sell
pantyhose without any change?
A customer unfurls a tale
of New Year's Eve hose-horror:
finding a hole near the butterfly
at her ankle when she put them on.
Her entire evening in shreds,
she wore a plain pair.
Hon, look at these snags –
you said you never wore them.
The verdict arrives:
See if there's another pair out.
(Wear them New Year's Eve,
bring them back and get a new pair –
why not?, they mutter.)
And just wait till they get their hands
on the girl who left them no change.

OTTÓ ORBÁN

Alban Berg: Opus 4, The Altenberg Songs

Schoenberg, Altenberg, Berg – a mountain-peak in all three
  names.
In other words our modern art is peaky.
So birdsong gives birth to dodecaphonics,
that logical cage in which there trills a canary with a diploma.
If you get to know the secrets of the trade, leave them at
  home,
work only from memory. The masterpiece is always
  accidental.
You need a slight touch of the dilettante
in order to believe in the sheeted ghost of absolute loneliness
which like a rusty hinge creaks at the door of the century . . .
Everything's against it, the fashion, Schoenberg himself;
in vain . . . In the jolly and bloody town of the king and the
  emperor
the elegant audience springs angrily to its feet to swat the
  composer –
forty more years before it learns what scrapes and billows
  like this,
what kind of wire glitters in the black smoke of damnation.

Night Call

This will be just like that crazy telephone call
before midnight in the tropics, in the hotel in Delhi;
I wake from a black sea that rocks the purring lifeboat
of the air-conditioning, I'm silver as a flying fish,
I speak neither English nor Hungarian,
only my splitting gills help me to bear the shower
of words, that begging, aggressive, otherworldly voice:
Come here at once, I want to sleep with you!
This will be the same, except I won't put down the receiver
or turn to the wall, but shall put on my shirt and trousers;
I know who it is, that oriental look cannot disguise her;
I've waited for you, the door opens, its hinges are centuries,

and her black hair glows with a blue flame and covers
  everything;
a thin line of smoke escapes through the keyhole, that was
  me . . .

Translated by George Szirtes.

GYÖRGY PETRI

Cemetery Plot No. 301

Let everything stay as it is!
With the carcasses from the Zoo?
Why, yes. Was their fate any different?
Was hanging any kinder than putting to sleep?
I cannot forget (when I say this,
I don't mean to threaten: it's the way I am:
I'm not able to forget).

On the other hand, what would I wish
for myself if I'd been – ha-ha! – hanged?
if I were to come back as a Stone Guest?
I'd wish at long last to be left in peace.
I shit on reverence. To these men
more mercy should've been shown when they were alive
(they should've been left alive). Now it's too late.

Against death there is no *remedium*.
No compensation for widows,
orphans, nations. I'm not interested
in the hangman's mate and his belated tears.
My eyes are dry. I need them for looking with.

Though actually there isn't much
to see – only, in the dusk
everything gets sharper:
a female body, a branch,
the downs of your face. I don't want
anything. Just to keep looking, no more.

Translators' note: When Nagy and his colleagues were hanged, their bodies were immediately dumped in a cemetery adjacent to the prison. Their grave, unmarked, was plot no.301. In June 1989, on the thirty-first anniversary of their deaths, the bodies were exhumed, coffined, given the full honours of a state funeral and reburied in plot no.301, now suitably memorialised. It was found, when the graves were first opened, that the bones of animals from a nearby zoo had been buried along with them.

Cold Peace

In the absence of peace, your plain man's mind might think:
there will be war. There being no war,
your learnèd mind would believe:
this now is peace. But it is and will be neither.

(1987)

Translated by Clive Wilmer & George Gömöri.

CHRISTOPHER PILLING

The elasticity of itness

The braces of the fictive café proprietor
are as potentially twangy as what I utter
when I come to realise the pebble I'm holding
could be, yes, one of Molloy's or the one that Golding
took to fashion his *Spire* with, building up from a nub
to a macrocosmic whole in the sky – with its hub
in a whirl (a whorl of deep significance). No mere
objective this or that! No more it! What if I shear
off all suggestive implications, start by ducking

all ultimate meanings? A special stone for sucking
's to be sucked, an ultra-phenomenological
fact. I'm holding a door handle and the logical
self feels the handle of a door in the grasping hand.
O.k. I feel nausea that I cannot understand.
My voice distorts. My and's become an ampersand, thus
creating its potential otherness, itness plus.

PETER PORTER

The Grand Old Tunes of Liberalism

They're the ones we never sang, we had it so good
but could always hear them through the decreed
miseries of classicism, the well-fee'd
alla marcias and symphonies of greed –
unheard melodies are sweeter, we understood.

All the great composers were heresiarchs
of happiness; they believed in it in notes
if not in lives, but a looking-out for votes
converted their long melodies to simple quotes
and Orpheus & Co's sound-bites in Sunday parks.

Just like the Church, the deeper thinkers held
that misery's modes and scales were Nature's voice
from the abyss, that modulation's choice
precluded choosing and equality was noise:
since Art was Fascist Nature must be as well.

But yet the notes kept going cancrizans,
insisting on imbuing the human mind
with a glory that it knew it left behind
in childhood – a sunburst for the blind
was the deaf composer's bequest to his fans.

It could never stay so even – back on earth
The Field of Folk turned out to be The Mob,
scholarship sat late assessing 'Blow Job,
an Epillion' and genius proved a snob –
everybody hummed the one tune from Perm to Perth.

And when they fed 'the self' in their computer
the songs of bards from Yeats to Murray warned
their Whigs that 'nothing's free when it's explained',
while on the screen the hero's new name dawned,
'Suburban Commando Mutant General Suitor.'

Today we're trapped in faceless symmetry
as the white noise of Demos disputes air-time
with the monkish runes of Heritage, when chime
is held a wonder and accident a rhyme
and faction shouts by the well-tempered sea.

Somewhere outlandish perhaps above the blast
or more probably beneath it, a human sound
continues, pain and joy on common ground,
the Liberalism our fathers thought they'd found,
a bridge-passage to the future from the past.

ZSUZSA RAKOVSZKY

Paper Boats

That time and circumstance are a foolproof
barrier . . . don't you believe that stuff!
Psychologically though . . .? Perhaps some truth
in that. At six, say, you practically fall off
the bridge with the cranky rail, leaning out

to see whether the paper boat you launched
three steps away on the far side has made it
safely through. And say it manages to ride
the darkly shadowed water, a branch may catch
it or the frothing miniature waterfall clutch
it to its white belly and drag it under –
but say it survives that too, and has scampered,
accelerating, practically keeling over,
to the black throat, the very threshold
of the arch of that black corridor where suds
of water pass beneath the ground, and with raised prow
moves under grass, stone, and earth although
its waterproof tinfoil has unwound, towards
the open waters, out of the stink of sewers
and into another town, where if you were
to arrive in your coat with its mangy fur
collar, no-one would mock you, saying, 'Who wears
such things nowadays?'; it wouldn't matter
if you took sugar in your tea, nor would you
have to quake in your boots while lying to
a squint-eyed schoolmarm with the face of a bloater
knowing she knows, if only in nightmares.
Purity and goodness must exist somewhere,
or what's a bleak life for? Possibilities
remain: you may launch your personal qualities
as often as you like on genuine seas.
An experienced stepmother may counterfeit
a well-loved parent in one's dreams, although
you can never quite decide precisely what
to call her: memory? or hope? It's hard to know.

Translated by George Szirtes.

PETER REDGROVE

A Passing Cloud

I.

They tell of thunder picked up on the teeth,
Or radio decoded on a filling, one's mouth
Buffeted with Sousa; but this was a dull ache
Pouring from a black cloud, I could get
No message from this broadcast, I must have
This radio pulled. 'No,' said my father,
'Keep your tooth, this is but a passing cloud.' I knew
It was him, because that was the brand
Of cigarettes he smoked, 'Passing Cloud' by Wills, and
'Yes,' he said abruptly, 'It's me,' and turned white;
By this token I knew he was dead,
Knew it again.

II.

When I had flu I always sweated his smell; his two wardrobes
Were exhaling it from hanging woollen shoulders like a last
     breath,
This ancient eighty-four-year-old sandalwood was his
     presence now,
It soaked into me and travelled home and stayed some days,
Grief like 'flu; but I could close my eyes and use it as an Inn
To meet up with this wayfarer and imagine him.

III.

The cat's way is to spray
And then rub her head in the odour
Like a beautiful woman admiring her mirror-image,
Her portrait thick-painted in impasto pheromones;
This is a cat of magic and she lives
In smell-spirit land as the makers of De Retzke
Printing a black cat on their packets, understand.
That was the other brand he used to smoke
Spraying the tinted air like ostrich feathers,

A chieftain's nose of nostril-plumes,
A rainmaker's cloud he passed, admiring
The sensation in the mirror of the smoke,
The sooth-ing oracle and breaker of time,
The redolent satisfaction that snaps the chain
Into peace and the smell of him
Smoking somewhere quietly in the house.

IV.
His presence fills the house when he is smoking,
His nature reaches into every cranny,
Into the carpets and eiderdowns and squads of suits;
The chain is broken now, finis,
And though I can smoke in his house now without consent
The smell of cigarettes does not bring him back,
As he is ashes and has been smoked and stubbed out
'A passing cloud . . .' so that time
For him never forges chains again.

V.
Except I notice that being under the weather
I sniff my hand-back and his scent appears; my whole skin
And atmosphere remembers him, the rain falls
And my toothache turns to tears, while the world fills
With reflecting mirror-water fathered out of rain-smells.

CHRISTOPHER REID

Epigone

The last sphinx in captivity
was a disappointing beast,
hardly worthy of the name –
with its unwholesome pelt
like a doubtful
jumble-sale bargain,
and wincing, bloodshot eyes.

67

All the same,
it was a genuine sphinx
and, once you'd tracked it
to its cage,
could still offer you,
if not some great
poetic riddle to solve,
then at least
a few fairly flabbergasting lies.

OLIVER REYNOLDS

Rilke: Change

For years he found it in looking.
Stars knelt
compelled by gazing.
Or he would kneel and his look
keen and sudden as scent
would weary the holy
worn down to sleep and a smile.

Looking made him
the terror of towers:
building them up again in a blink!
And yet often at evening a landscape,
exhausted by day, would come to rest
in the stillness of being watched.

Animals calmly flocked
to the open pastures of the look
and the lions in their cage
stared unseeing into the freedom within them;
birds flew through it,
direct as thought; flowers
returned the look, growing
as huge as they are to children.

And the rumour there was one who could see
reached those who are less
easily seen,
reached women.

How long can looking last?
How many years now of utter need
crying from the soul of the eye?

Waiting was second nature to him, absently sitting
in the neutral disorder of a hotel room
with its back turned on him, a hotel room
skulking in the shunned mirror
and later, from his sleepless bed,
the same scene:
the air summing up,
summing up out of earshot
the state of his living heart,
entombed in the pain of his body
his still living heart
was summed up and judged:
it was loveless.

(And compassion cancelled all claim on him.)
Look, then, at the limits of looking.
And at the seen world's need
to be nurtured by love.

The eye's work is over,
now work with the heart
on the images imprisoned within:
forcibly yours, they're now unknown to you.
Let the man within you look at the woman there,
this one found
among thousands, this being
at first only found, still
to be loved.

STEPHEN ROMER

Fin de Règne

On the fringes
of their sheeted palace
a brother and sister
fret the summer out

in shorts and flip-flops.
The brother shows us round,
a bashful-proud
curator of his childhood,

skirting the severities
of antique chairs,
poker-backed chaperones
long since glorified.

Obscurely come down
from the Knights of St John
he's overlooked
by a frieze of ancestors

gestured at
by religiose painting.
A Mannerist Christ
elaborately deposed

excites approval
from our languid host;
he drops his hand
and shuffles on,

his supine nasals
out of England
projecting
through the stonedust . . .

'Salvatore Rosa
probably,
but we've never bothered . . .
This vaulting's very rare';

a deprecating whinny.
The limestone ceiling
is a casket lid
seen from below.

Down in the cellar
some withered balloons
remind him
of the olden days

and his mouth
almost puckers
at the wreckage
of his German trainset

under a landslide
of cratered masonry.
One floor up,
Technics Lego

has inherited
the patio;
his sister's son
by a marine husband

is building an airport
without a runway.
Plump, boisterous,
he whoops in the trees.

The Idolator

Who can survive
the stare of the idolator . . .

Like Rappaccini
he'd have perfection

even at the price of death,
smoothing her to marble

with his eyes.
What blemish

could deceive that scrutiny,
what flesh?

ANNE ROUSE

Nightside

When a body's anger
Sharpens to sex;
When the brain's bestiary
Resolves to it,
And from the furthest
Lake – a caldera
Between mountains –
Thrusts upwards, dripping,
This,
Then who dreams
Of the one warm beside?

But if that one goes,
And the horizon
Torques and twists,
Widdershins,
So that the known world
Flips, what
Does a body do, but sink
In dreaming's furrow,
As if the past's
Warm reek returns
At sorrow?

CAROL RUMENS

Sans Souci Park, Belfast

an English view

I am my neighbours' lives, their woodwork parties,
The war-dance of their lusts, their shoe grenades,
The no-surrender dialogue of their doors.

My head's the hollow kitchen where their Hotpoint
Beats the wash all night, and gender governs
Their quarrels in remorseless stereotype.

And what am I to them? An ancient deafness
Under their floorboards, self-preserved and foreign.
I was an oak-tree but I've started shaking.

I couldn't name them, recognise their faces,
Yet listening to them's now my one obsession.
In this I'm an example to my country.

In Memory of a Friendship

Winter has reached the Spanish Steps, advancing
On tides of dirty suds like the landlady
Who mopped her way past literature, enticing
Tubercle bacilli from every mouse-hole.
The red street-carpets, weeping muddily,
Persuade the tourists to the Latin Quarter.
Hawkers, pipers, backpackers, gypsies, thieves,
Unabashed by the civic or the tonal,
Go on arguing as they've always done.
If a poet's down to his last adjective,
They know as much about it as the rain.

Joseph takes the day off for gardening.
He'd mentioned violets, and his friend forgot
The taste of coughed-up rust, fed on their sweetness.
The gifts seem lame, now, curiously weightless,
Loveletters to a sickbed, crushed unopened.
His own hand clenches, but he crowds the plot.
The buds twist on their necks to look at him,
Measure his skewed perspective, his unquickened
Muse. These were his painting-days. The rest
Is a double-grave, much visited, but modest,
The young men in it sharing, like two students,
Who think they've all their fame ahead of them.

Now sunlight soothes the convalescent steps
Where the tourists never leave, but simply swap
Countries, friends and occasionally, their jeans.
Epiphany's over, and the filthy carpets
Rolled and trucked away to be drycleaned.
The landlady mops the hall again, re-lets
The rooms to the one tenant who'll never leave.
The rooms learn to be quiet. But youth can't learn.
It takes offence at barely lived-in bones,
Watches, distraught, its ownerless name become
Less than the rain, less than the grave that drowns
Each spring, in earth-rich violets, acts of love.

JO SHAPCOTT

Tom and Jerry Visit England

O boy, I thought. A chance
to visit England and O boy here, out
of nowhere, a voice to describe it. Reader,
I dreamt of coming back to tell you how I marched
round the Tower of London, in a beefeater suit,
swished my axe at Jerry, belted after him
into the Bloody Tower, my back legs
circling like windmills in a gale
while ravens flapped around our heads.
You would hear it all: tea with the Queen
at Buckingham Palace and me scattering
the cucumber sandwiches at the sight
of Jerry by the silver salver. I couldn't wait
for the gorgeous tableau: Queenie with her mouth
in a little shocked screaming shape, her crown
gone crooked as she stood cringing on the throne
with her skirts up round her knees, and Jerry
down there laughing by the footstool.
I would be a concertina zig-zag by that time
with a bone china cup stuffed in my face
and a floral tea pot shoved on my head so hard
my brains would form a spout and a handle
when it cracked and dropped off.

I can't get this new voice to explain to you
the ecstasy in the body when you fling
yourself into such mayhem, open yourself
to any shape at all and able to throw out
stars of pain for everyone to see.

But reader, the visit wasn't like that.
I ended up in a poem and it made me uneasy.
Cats prefer to skulk and sulk
in the dark, we prefer mystery

and slinking. This is even true of me
with my stupid human face opening
into only two or three stupid expressions:
cunning, surprise and maybe rage.
And I couldn't find Jerry.

'Where's the mouse?' I tripped
over commas and colons hard like diamonds, looking
for him. 'Where's the mouse?' I kept asking,
'Where's the mouse?' I banged full face into a query –
and ended up with my front shaped
like a question mark for hours. That was scary:
I usually pop right back into myself in seconds.
So I hesitated for once before flinging myself
down the bumpy staircase where all the lines ended.

I went on my rear and at the bottom you would have seen me,
end up, bristling with splinters, and nose down
snuffling for any trace of mouse smell.
Reader, it was my first tragic movie:
I couldn't find the mouse.

The Mad Cow Tries to Write the Good Poem

The police came once when I was doing my death dance
to the amazing circular music which had entered a gap
near my cortex and acted as powerfully as a screwdriver
on my soul. I wove in and out of the green trees. I used
my hooves as gentle weapons in the air. A bit of newspaper
fame came my way that day, but shit, it was a performance
ephemeral, and certainly not the good poem. Lasting.
How can I last when I live in a shed and even
the postman doesn't know how to find me?
It's dark in here. Light would echo the gaps
in my brain coils and set off a fizzing reaction,
not so much pounding, more an explosion
followed by a flowing moment when the taboo

people arrive. They're dressed in red and
stand formally around my skull as though staged
for an opera. And when they sing—sometimes as many
as seven at once—then, friend, please, the good
poem is sounding all round this hut, my head, the world,
I hear it written in the streaky emulsion on the walls,
in my own messing on the floor, in the nation's smeary dailies,
in lovely people's ears, their breath, your breath:
it's new every time, always wanted and easy to spot
because I know what it looks like with my eyes closed.

LOUIS SIMPSON

Working Out

A middleaged man named Doherty
had the locker next to mine.
A detective. He showed me
scar tissue near his heart
where a bullet had gone in.

A new member joined, a woman
who was doing physiotherapy.
She was beautiful to watch
at Leg Curl and Leg Extension,
straddling a seat or lying down.

The tone of the whole place changed.
When she came, Doherty would run over
and be solicitous:
how was she feeling today,
and she mustn't overdo it.

Then she no longer came, she was cured,
and everything reverted:
the young men blowdrying their hair
assiduously, the old
telling their dirty stories.

77

And Doherty working out
at Pullover, Double Chest,
and Torso Arm . . . lifting weights
as though it were he or they
in a struggle to the death.

ANNE STEVENSON

Washing the Clocks

Time to go to school, cried
the magnifying lens of the alarm clock.
Time to go home now, the school's
Latin numerals decided.
Days into weeks, months into years.

At last it's time thoroughly to wash
the outsides and insides of the clocks.

They've lined themselves up on the dresser,
worn out, submitting patiently.
The old woman in her yellow head-square
prepares to take them apart.

First she pries the glass off the black clock.
The glow-painted arabics fade as she scrubs.
Now a faint fringe of dawn stars
freckles the licked black dish.

Next, with a little lead key, she
applies herself to the school clock.
Tears must have rusted the hinge.
She has to force the case open . . .
Two pointed swords and a needle
clatter to the tessellated floor.

Where have they gone? Well, look for them!
Feel for the hands in the dust,
in the blowing sand. Finger by finger
the numerals break off and drop down.

My terror is yours and everyone's,
but the woman is blind, evidently,
and takes no note of her loss.
How competently she's removing
the scarred blank face of my old school clock.

Behind it, the whirring machine –
gleaming brass rods and revolving cogs
keeping time all by themselves,
rinsing the mesh of their wheels in mysterious oil.

MATTHEW SWEENEY

After Closing Time

*'Those who don't believe in life after death should be here
after closing time.': notice inside an office in Derry's city
cemetery.*
The gate will be open, and streetlights
will guide you through the graves,
but you'd better watch your carry-outs
as the dead are barred from pubs.
Watch for the flowers that fly
from grave to grave, creating letters
for the papers and maybe more dead –
and one thing you'll know in the half-light
is that the dead are too many
to fit in the ground, too lively
to lie in a box, so they do
what you'd expect them to, and that's why
they surround you as you swig
from a can. They ruffle your hair,

breathe through unbrushed teeth,
fart even, and one of the pushier
puts his finger in the hole in his head
then invites you to follow. Another
opens his rotting shirt to show you
his two hearts, the old and the new,
and a one-legged ex-pensioner
eyes the bulge of your cigarettes,
and you'd be well advised to drain
one can, then chuck the other
as far as you're able, for the dead
hate those who outlive them,
and you'd be canny to suss this
and run, and hope the gate's not shut.

GEORGE SZIRTES

Inuit

I have fallen in love with this baby
whose empty eyes and wrinkled mouth
appear to be essence of baby,
his death a perfect pathos
without sentiment, still as a photograph
of stillness, without potential energy,
with how he looks and does not look at me.

Could he be the Christchild, under an Eskimo moon,
part moon himself with pitted eyes,
proverbial round cheese, a comforting thing
in uncomforting space, registering surprise
at the thingness of anything and everything?
And why is he more touching than any live baby?
More nocturnal, more animal? And might he wake up soon?

I hit a deer once, doing a steady lick
at dead of night. Its quivering body
was a thousand startled eyes. I didn't see him fall
but felt his dark soft leg, a heavy stick,
hammer briefly at my metal sheath
then disappear as we sped on, unable
to adjust to his appearance, or
the knowledge of his death.

It was on the brow of a hill. We were heading north,
the notional arctic, but would later bend east
toward Norfolk as the sky lightened. I want to speak light
for the baby, that he might understand. Let him at least
hear the noise of our passage over the earth
and watch the live deer crashing out of sight.

The Baths On Monroe Street

At the baths on Monroe Street two women are crying.
The walls are patched and blistered like Eliot's Jew.
Decades of steam. The carpet is wet through
With feet or with tears and the matrons are dying
Of cancer or disappointment, their hair crimped in sheets,
Their broad bosoms swaying over stomachs arranged in pleats.

In a sudden fury Alice begins. She launches a volley
Of clicks at the mist and the leery disappearing
Smiles of a hundred Cheshire Cats who may be hard of hearing
But know an assault when they see one. Like a reveille
The cry goes up to wake the dead, and the dead rise
Out of the walls and the water with terrible answering cries.

Ah love let us be true to one another! they wail in the steam
Of the baths, remembering their Matthew Arnold. The
   towels snap
As they descend on the savage intruder, the teeth also snap,
And the air's full of flesh. They can see the gleam
Of the lens, which is Alice in action, and they close in
As all nightmares do, on those who are rigid or frozen.

They take the instrument from her (and who, after all
Can blame them? Because theirs is a life not to be opened
Like a tin of sardines, because they feel they own what has
   happened
And goes on happening to them as they totter and fall
On the slippery carpet) and by the time their energies fail
The camera is drowned in a cleaner's convenient pail.

CHARLES TOMLINSON

The Improvement

                The hallway once
   Ran straight through the house, and you could see
Entrance to exit in one sweep
   Of the eye across a cobbled floor –
Unexplored, the territory of the rooms
   To either side. One day
It was resolved to block that shaft
   With a vestibule, and to curb its tendency
With a further jut of wall half way.
   Do I like the changes? A ghost
Could not pass straight through
   Without confusion now. What ghost, you say?
The ghost that is my memory which quickens still
   At the thought of the long passage lit
From door to door, the clean
   Flight of the senses through it, like a wife
Running to meet her man, like a bird's flight, a life.

JOHN WHITWORTH

A Language Lesson

I used to sit with Colin, my fat friend,
Backs to the wall and bums well off the pitch,
(Your immigrant is well advised to blend).
Mad *fitba'* raged before us, end to end
From blazered railings down to the *kludgie*, which

Is Scots for lavatory, as I called ours
Where I studied English County Cricket scores
In tame defiance. Scottish Colin's fat
Was existential – he ate Bounty Bars
While catechizing me on this and that.

Going the messages means shopping, *roan*
Means drainpipe, rolls are *baps*, and alley's *vennel*.
Your Scot'll never tease. He *tak's a loan*
O' donnert folk – whit sort o' folk, ye ken, 'll
Be toffee-nosed (with accents like my own).

I hammered at it nightly in my prayers:
Please God, make me pure Scots in word and deed.
And God is good. Now, if I cross the Tweed,
I feel the blood within me rise, *Here's tae us*
Wha's like us? Bluidy few, an' they're a' deid.

(Via Birmingham it happens at Carstairs.)

SUSAN WICKS

Black and White

Old Russian woman,
arms like exposed roots,
mouth one level line of shadow,
she stands,
not noticing the petals,
not noticing the clouds,
outstaring the camera,
blossom-drift over her,
freak snowstorm in lush grass,
May-winter.

Because she is old and in black
the May-blizzard shows up on her,
freckled and full of birth as an egg.

HUGO WILLIAMS

Sealink

On the boat, we foot passengers
were shuffled like a pack of cards
and thrown down in new combinations
all over the half-empty, off-season decks.
Children bumped into one another.
Parents looked for somewhere quiet to sit
away from the video games.
Young couples ate enormous, nervous meals,
while single people roamed back and forth
between the restaurant and Duty Free.

As land came into sight, one asked another
'Do you know the way back to the coach?
I think it's on Whale Deck.'

A conversation begins with 'May I sit
next to you? God it's hot in here!
Do you mind if I open this window?'
We take off our coats, settle back, peel oranges.
Shall we speak in English or French?
Are we going on holiday? Or home?
Do we mind knowing each other's name?

Amtrak

Americans have left their things out to rust
beside the river Hudson. Cars and cranes and sheds
lie buried in toxic foam near Roxy's Lighthouse.
LIQUID FLO-SWEET – SUGAR FOR INDUSTRY
rolls backwards down THE ROUTE OF THE VISTA
DOME.

'If you care to look out the window for a moment,
this here is the Mohawk Valley we're entering.'
Our ancient ticket-collector passes down the car.
'He was in the papers not long ago,' says my neighbour.
'They were doing a series on the last of the patriots.'

GERARD WOODWARD

The House Croesus Built

Would you really
Want to live in this
Ingot, when all

Who leave leave richer?
Touch it and your
Fingers are small fortunes.

Yes, its roof holds off
Rainy days, but for how much
Longer, when the plumber cuts

Out good pipes
And guests hawk
Light bulbs through jewellers,

Or even pinch cobwebs
To give as gifts from this
Bright and famous house?

In a month the stairs have worn
To what it takes a church
Four hundred years,

And vague footprints
Lead everywhere. No bank
To deposit this,

It is its own soft fort
And who can steal a building?
Enough unknowing burglars

Can. The friction of visitors
Means it's thinning fast,
And when the walls start

To buckle, and the last glare
Of dust is carried off on soles,
Will the secret bullion

Of its foundations really
Give the worms their luggage,
So they drag down its riches, millionaires?